D0463771

Moments for Sisters

by Robert Strand

First printing, January 1996
Seventh printing, January 2006

ISBN: 0-89221-302-7
Library of Congress Catalog Number: 95-69898

Cover design by Left Coast Design, Portland, OR.

All Scripture references are from the New International Version, unless otherwise noted.

New Leaf Press
A Division of New Leaf Publishing Group
www.newleafpress.net

Printed in China

Presented to:

_____

Presented by:

_____

Date:

_____

Day 1
How to Torture Your Sister

• SHE ate her jelly doughnut at lunch. You saved yours. It is now two hours later:

Sit down next to your sister on the couch. Put the jelly doughnut on a napkin in your lap. Leave it, untouched, until she asks you if you still want it. Then begin eating. "Mmmm. This is soooo good." Take a large bite and chew with mouth open so she gets a good view. Swallow and run tongue over lips. "Mmmm." Stick tongue in jelly center and wave it around in the air before pulling it back in mouth. "Don't you wish you had some?" Take tiny bites. Lick fingers in between. "Boy . . . there's nothing like having a jelly doughnut in the middle of the afternoon!" Pop last bite in mouth and pat stomach.

• WANDER into the room when she calls a friend on the telephone. Pick up a book and sit down on the couch. Pretend to read, then mimic her as she begins her telephone conversation.

Hi, how are you? *Hi, how are you?* Wha'd you do today? *Wha'd you do today?* What? Wait a minute, my sister's driving me crazy. Would you cut it out. *Would you cut it out.* You dirty creep. *You dirty creep.* Stop repeating me! *Stop repeating me!* I'll kill you if you don't stop! *I'll kill you if you don't stop!* I said STOP! *I said STOP!* STOP IT!! *STOP IT!!*

Put down book and run.

- SHE is eating peanuts. Whisper in her ear, "You can turn into an elephant if you eat too many peanuts. I read it in the *World Book*."
- FOLLOW her everywhere.
- IMITATE her best friend talking. Say that her best friend is fat.
- TALK to your mother while your sister is listening: "Do you remember Christmas when I was three years old and you gave me that stuffed animal? That was so much fun." Turn to your sister: "You weren't alive."
- YOU are in bed with the flu, watching television. She has been told to keep out of your room so that she doesn't catch it, too. As she walks by the door, stare goggle-eyed at the TV: "Oh my goodness! That's incredible! I've never seen anything like it in my life! I can't believe it! Wait till I tell the kids at school." Do not remove eyes from set, staring in amazement. "I wouldn't miss this for anything! I really don't believe it." Look at your sister. "What?" Move over on the bed. "Of course there's room for you."*

*Delia Ephron, *How to Eat Like a Child* (New York, NY: Penguin USA, 1988).

Today's Quote: *Having a sister means having one of the most beautiful and unique of human relationships.*

Today's Verse: Isn't her younger sister more attractive? (Judg. 15:2).

Day 2
The Delany Sisters

Sarah and A. Elizabeth Delany, 104 and 106 (in 1994; Sarah has since passed away), have taken the reading public by storm. It was their surprise bestseller, *Having Our Say: The Delany Sisters' First 100 Years* that elevated them to become "America's grandmas." Charming, candid, witty, humorous, and wise, these sisters struck something in the souls of Americans that kept them on the *New York Times* best-seller list for 28 weeks! "Not bad for two old inky-dinks over 100 years old!" Bessie is fond of joking. These two have become one of the most famous pairs of sisters in America. They are delightful and easy to read.

As a result of all that attention, the letters have come pouring in from readers crammed with questions. People want their advice on all kinds of subjects . . . what to do was a problem. One day it dawned on them that they could write another book which would not give their life story but their secrets of old age. So in 1994 another book was released, *The Delany Sisters' Book of Everyday Wisdom* (with Amy Hill Hearth), which makes for fascinating fun reading.*

What is the secret of attaining old age? According to Sadie: "Well, start with this: No smoking, no drinking, no chewing. And always clean your plate. We get up with the sun, and the first thing we do is exercise. God gave you only one body, so you better be nice to it. Exercise, because if you don't, by the time you're our age, you'll be pushing up daisies."

According to Bessie: "I have gotten smarter about a few things in my old age, things like taking chances. Now, I know there are folks who are afraid to try anything new, and that's a big problem for them. But me, I was never afraid of anything. I mean, I was always absolutely fearless! Naturally that meant that I didn't always have good sense."

From them both: "For about the last 35 years, things were mighty quiet. We had a pleasant life, working in the garden, going to church, visiting with friends and neighbors. We took good care of ourselves, doing exercises . . . except Sunday . . . and eating carefully. We eat a whole lot of vegetables and fruits and take vitamin supplements.

"Now it seems like the whole world has been writing to us . . . it seems that a lot of folks, especially young ones, don't know how to live right. We're as old as Moses, so maybe we have learned a few things along the way, and we'd like to pass them on. We hope you find them useful."*

*Amy Hill Hearth, *The Delany Sisters' Book of Everyday Wisdom* (New York, NY: Kodansha International, 1994).

Today's Quote: *God was the center of our Christian home.* — Sadie and Bessie Delany

Today's Verse: "Honor your father and mother" — which is the first commandment with a promise — "that it may go well with you and that you may enjoy long life on the earth" (Eph. 6:2–3).

Day 3
The Delaney Sisters, II

SADIE: For us there was never a time when we did not believe in God. There's a lot in this world you can't see that you still believe in, like love and courage. Well, that's the way it is with faith. Just because you can't hold it in your hand doesn't mean it's not there. A person who has faith is prepared for life and to do something with it.

The Word of God . . . was the center of our home. The Bible is where we go for guidance. God's wisdom is at work in the words, but you can also get plenty of practical advice in the Bible. After all, mankind hasn't changed that much.

BESSIE: When we walk into our house . . . whether we're coming back from a long trip or just from seeing the neighbors . . . the first thing we say is, "We're home. Praise the Lord." We do that to honor Him, to thank Him for watching over us.

I think God understands that I'm only human. He gave this mouth, He gave me a temper, and so I'm bound to err. I'm sure I must be getting credit for trying! But every once in a while, just to keep on His path, I try to take in an old-fashioned fire-and-brimstone sermon. I'm an Episcopalian, and I appreciate the thoughtful preaching in my church . . . but there's nothing like fire and brimstone to set me straight. Fight fire with fire, I always say!

SADIE: I can't get over the litter on the ground in New York City. People eat a sandwich, they throw the wrapper on the ground. You might think that's a little thing to be provoked about, but it's not a little thing. It shows a lot about the character of the person, that he doesn't care about any one else. It's plain bad manners!

We hate bad manners. By "manners" I don't mean using the right fork or spoon at the dinner table. All I'm talking about is performing simple acts of consideration, which sounds easy . . . and it is easy, but too few people even bother to try.

BESSIE: When you get older, it's natural to look back on your life. And like most folks, I have a few regrets. The main regrets I have from 100 years of living come from when I haven't treated someone as well as I could have. And I can be a little mean. Sadie never says anything mean about anyone, especially if they're dead.

Mama used to tell me, "Bessie, someday you're going to have to account for every mean thing you've ever said." That's what's got me so worried. If I had to do it all over again, I'd hush up once in a while.

Today's Quote: *When it comes to money, keep your mouth shut.* — Sadie & Bessie Delany

Today's Verse: Listen to your father, who gave you life, and do not despise your mother when she is old (Prov. 23:22).

Day 4
My Mother's Sisters

In the early part of my childhood I did not know any of my relatives because they lived in Nova Scotia, 2,000 miles away. My parents had left Nova Scotia during the Depression because there were no jobs there. My two aunts were very much present in the spirit. The three sisters wrote one another every week, and my mother read these letters out loud after dinner. They were called "letters from home."

It was not my invisible aunts in their present-day incarnation who made the most impression on me — it was my aunts in the past. There they were as children, in the starched and frilled dresses and the floppy satin hair bows of the first decades of the century, or as shingle-haired teenagers, in black and white in the photograph album, wearing strange clothing, cloche hats, flapper coats up over the knee, standing beside antique motor cars, or posed by the sea in striped bathing suits that came halfway down their legs. Sometimes their arms would be around one another. My mother gave them captions, in white pencil on the black album pages: "We Three," "Bathing Belles."

Aunt J. was thin as a child, dark-eyed, intense. Aunt K., the middle sister, looked tailored and brisk, in a Dutch cut. My mother, with huge pre-Raphaelite eyes and wavy hair and models' cheekbones, was the beauty, an assessment she made light of. All three sisters had the same high-bridged noses; Roman noses, my mother said. I pored over these pictures, intrigued by the identical noses. I did not have a sister myself, then, and the mystique of sisterhood was potent for me.*

If you were to spend time around sisters, likely you would discover the ones who are the closest shared several things in common . . . parents had been committed to making sure that their daughters would be friends, a high regard for each other, respect for the other, felt as though they were equals regardless of other factors, and when a sister was in need the other became the caregiver. Just knowing that a sister is there at all times is a great comfort. The continual sharing, the can't-wait-to-tell-my-sister, is part of the bonding between sisters. It's a relationship that is not to be taken lightly.

*Margaret Atwood, *Family Portraits: Remembrances of Twenty Celebrated Writers* (New York, NY: Bantam, Doubleday, Dell Pub. Group, Inc., 1989).

Today's Quote: *One's sister is a part of one's essential self, an eternal presence of one's heart and soul and memory.* — Susan Cahill

Today's Verse: She had a sister called Mary, who sat at the Lord's feet listening to what he said (Luke 10:39).

You can't think how I depend on you, and when you're not there the colour goes out of my life.

Virginia Woolf

Day 5
Sisters

We had the usual fights and bickering as children, but once we reached our teenage years my sister and I left all that behind. I can't remember a quarrel between us after we were grown. Everyone agreed we were almost clones of each other, with mutual passions for cooking, sewing, and singing. I always wanted to have the red hair and green eyes Sharon was born with; she envied the blond hair and blue eyes I inherited.

She always said I had the "brains," but after her children were grown she attended college and became an accomplished bookkeeper. I admired her flair for nourishing and loving not only her own, but also a number of foster children, and also the strength to relinquish her place in their lives when the time came. We always celebrated each other's accomplishments and steps forward with a total lack of jealousy or envy, and we bore each other's hurts as though they were our own.

But our sisterhood was cut short by her early death due to many medical problems. She had cancer and conquered it — remaining free of it 12 years after the surgery that removed it. But she was also diabetic, and that disease followed her with a vengeance beyond its usual limits. The far-reaching effects of it finally caused kidney failure, near-blindness, and eventually, death at the age of 45. However, even that could not obliterate the intertwining of our lives. The memories live on; they even continue to be made.

This sister thing even transcends generations. I revel in the accomplishments of her children, and the joy of the arrival of each of her grandchildren. Many times her children and mine blend to celebrate a holiday. It's a normal "family" thing to do, but there is an underlying grasp at continuity that makes it more. It's as though a part of her "motherhood" has been passed on to me. Her children know it, and I know it, but it's a gentle, subliminal thing of which we never speak.

Ten years after her death I still cannot eat a patty melt (Sharon's favorite) without a lump forming in my throat — in fact, I have even stopped trying. Sometimes when I'm flipping through my recipe cards and I come to one in her own handwriting, my heart does a double thump. When something remarkable (or unremarkable) happens in my life, I even yet occasionally think, *I must call Sharon.*

Yes, my sister was my soulmate and filled a part of my heart that no one else ever could. But there is no void — she is still there.

Today's Quote: *It is best to be with those in time we hope to be with in eternity.* — Sir Thomas Fuller

Today's Verse: In my Father's house are many rooms; if it were not so, I would have told you. I am going there to prepare a place for you (John 14:2).

Day 6
Sisterhood

Of all the many relationships that are part of a woman's life, the bonds between sisters are unique. Sisterhood is stretching, bending, whether close at hand or from a distance, but very rarely breaking. The ties that bind sisters together seem to be plagued by less relational knots than mothers and daughters. Sisters at one and the same time can be girlfriends, listening ears, best friends, shopping collaborators, just plain buddies, confidantes, rivals, and much, much more.

Some research studies show that older women who have strong sister relationships are less likely to become depressed than the women who don't have a sister. One of these studies uncovered the fact that many women felt the world was a safer place because their sisters would be there in times of crisis. Sisters, whatever you may say or think, function as one of the best support-systems/safety-nets in a world churned by the chaos of change all around us. Just the fact that a sister will be there is great comfort.

Now take brothers, they share the same biological links with each other . . . but they are so different. Brothers don't seem to have that same kind of emotional glue holding them together as sisters. Sisters are different from brothers in that sisters have something very intimate . . . a sharing of a soul, something that brothers are not usually open enough to obtain.

The memories for sisters are better than brothers . . . sharing a bathtub together, goodnight kisses and snuggles, watching each other's bodies grow, who had the first period, the one who never gains weight, who is aging better, who has more wrinkles, and so on. The memories extend beyond the same roof to social milestones . . . always boyfriends, competition, clothes wars, shopping sprees, dance lessons, cheerleading, pompoms, first solo, music contests, marching bands, and family picnics. Then there are the emotional memories . . . advice whispered, loyalty that cannot be broken, phone calls that are endless in length, going to church together, being Daddy's little girl, who is getting the most attention, who might be Mom's favorite, and always, who is rejected.

Sisterhood is the interweaving of life lessons that are funny, happy, angry, and hurtful, and such memories build the foundation on which the very special, unique, and wonderful relationship of sisterhood rests and is built.

Today's Quote: *For there is no friend like a sister in calm and stormy weather; To cheer one on the tedious way, To fetch one if one goes astray, To lift one if one totters down, To strengthen whilst one stands.* — Christina Rosetti

Today's Verse: Jesus loved Martha and her sister (John 11:5).

Day 7
She's Still with Me

Since O.J. Simpson was accused of murdering his former wife, Nicole Brown Simpson, and her friend Ronald Goldman, we were riveted by the media to one of the most spectacular murder trials in recent history. The real truth will probably never be known.

What kind of an effect has this had on Nicole's oldest sister, Denise Brown? In an interview, she has expressed herself very freely and is dedicated to stopping domestic violence. In fact, the family has started a foundation in Nicole's memory which people can call to get information, talk to a volunteer, or make a donation. According to Denise, "We've gotten literally thousands of calls so far. I've got men in jail writing me letters saying, 'Please send me information because I'm here for abusing my wife and I really want some help.'"

Denise said, "...when I go to the cemetery, I get this burst of energy. I can see clearly, and I can think clearly; she's with me all the time."

The question was asked, "What have you learned about domestic violence?" Denise responded with, "If it happened once, it can happen again. My advice to women in that situation is to get out. But I'm as guilty as the next person. You don't do something until something tragic happens. And unfortunately it had to happen to my sister."

When asked, "If you could talk to Nicole one more time, what would you say?" Denise replied, "Come back. I just wish I could see her one last time. But I'm glad that when we left that last evening, I told her that I loved her. For that I'm grateful."

"Did Nicole have a favorite poem or prayer?" The answer from sister Denise was, "It was a poem called 'Morning Prayer,' by Ogden Nash. Nicole gave it to my son for his first Holy Communion.

> Now another day is breaking.
> Sleep was sweet but so is waking.
> Dear Lord, I promised you last night
> Never again to sulk or fight.
> Such vows are easier to keep
> When a child is sound asleep.
> Today, O Lord, for your dear sake,
> I'll try to keep them when awake.

She wrote in the book: "Sean, I hope you read and reread these beautiful prayers until you understand God's plan. . . . Happy first Communion. I'm so proud of you. Love, CoCo. May 7, 1994."*

*Melina Gerosa, *Ladies Home Journal*, 4/95, adapted.

Today's Quote: *What people need to do, what families need to do, is get involved. And this is what I wish I had known.* — Denise Brown

Today's Verse: This is what the Sovereign Lord says: "You will drink your sister's cup, a cup large and deep" (Ezek. 23:32).

Day 8
Beating the Blues

What do you do when your sister comes to you out of great sorrow, or from dealing with feelings of loneliness, hurting from the fall-out of grief, fighting depression, or just deep into a funk? How about sharing one or all of these "blue-mood-beaters." Perhaps you'll discover they will work for you as well as a sister:

1) It's maybe too simple . . . but start with asking God for strength to overcome this mood you find yourself stuck in.

2) Follow that by saying to yourself, "Self, I've been here before, felt this way before. It did not come to stay, it came to pass." The hurt or pain may not leave permanently . . . but the present mood often lifts.

3) Deliberately switch your thinking. Shift from unhappiness to one of those pleasant memories of growing up, put something pleasant into the thought mill. Change your mind from the negative to the positive.

4) Take a long walk. Weed the garden. Shovel the walks. Rake the leaves. Bathe the dog. Wash the car. Do something outside. If that's impossible, do something active indoors.

5) Count your present blessings. Even get out a sheet of paper and begin to list all of your present blessings, your past blessings, and what you anticipate as blessings in the future.

6) Help someone else who might be in worse condition than you are. Find a neighbor, a friend, a sister, a relative. Go to a nursing home . . . read to someone. Get out of your shell of self-pity and place yourself in a positive way in somebody else's.

7) Check to be sure this particular mood is not caused by a physical reason. Do something brave that sisters will do, go see your doctor for help.

8) Have the confidence that if you have really placed yourself in God's care — that someone or something will come along to help you through your mood or test or trial. Believe that God will help you deal with the unthinkable, bear the unbearable.

9) It helps to remember that every other person you meet has also had to deal with some of the tough problems of life, been depressed, been hurt, been lonely, been grieving. And some of these have not had the many tools available to you to cope with their needs. Take heart!

10) Believe that tomorrow will be a better day! Have faith in the future! Have faith in God! Have faith in relationships! Believe it!

Today's Quote: *While I know myself as a creation of God, I am also obligated to realize and remember that everyone else and everything else are also God's creation.* — Maya Angelou

Today's Verse: God has said, "Never will I leave you; never will I forsake you." So we say with confidence, "The Lord is my helper; I will not be afraid" (Heb. 13:5–6).

Day 9
Heaven Has a Face

Two young women, sisters for the hours they were to spend together in labor and childbirth, both prepared for the births of their first children. They were, after childbirth, placed in hospital rooms across the corridor from each other. The one mother-to-be had eagerly looked forward to and had planned for this blessed event. She and her husband had prepared a nursery, bought baby clothes, soft blankets, disposable diapers, and everything else that the newborn could possibly need. But, regardless of this thought and anticipation . . . this baby girl was stillborn. The doctor expressed to these hurting, grieving parents his heart-felt sympathy.

This young mother-to-be was crushed, broken, and became bitter! "Why? Why?" she cried.

Across the hall, this sister in labor and childbirth didn't want her baby, had made no plans other than to give her baby away. Knowing this only embittered the mother whose baby had died. She went home, depressed, angry at the world, at the doctors, at the hospital, and angry at God.

"Why, oh why, did my baby have to die?" she cried.

Then in Sunday school one Sunday, she picked up a child's story paper and in it read the simple story of a shepherd and his sheep and the efforts to get them to cross a stream.

The frustrated shepherd attempted to drive them across, but it was fruitless. He tried to lead them across, but to no avail. The sheep were too fearful of the running water.

Finally, the shepherd picked up a tiny lamb in his arms and with the little lamb held tight, he waded across the stream. The mother ewe, hearing the bleating of her little lamb across the stream, walked into the water and on over to the other side, and all the other sheep followed.

This young mother, who had lost her child, who had grown so bitter, in that moment began to see some kind of a reason for her loss. It dawned on her that the Lord, the Good Shepherd, had taken her little lamb across to the other side. Her reasons and resolve to follow Him became greater than before. Her little lamb was in heaven . . . she knew it. From that moment on, heaven was no longer some strange, hazy place out there . . . no, her baby was over there! Heaven was not so far removed, now. Heaven now had meaning, substance, someone she knew and loved. Heaven now has the face of her baby over there.

Today's Quote: *Where love reigns, the very joy of heaven itself is felt.*
— Hannah Hurnard

Today's Verse: As a shepherd looks after his scattered flock when he is with them, so will I look after my sheep. I will rescue them from all the places where they were scattered on a day of clouds and darkness (Ezek. 34:12).

Day 10
Four of a Kind

Margaret . . . the eldest of the four, was 16, and very pretty, being plump and fair, with large eyes, plenty of soft, brown hair, a sweet mouth, and white hands, of which she was rather vain.

Fifteen-year-old Jo was very tall, thin and brown, and reminded one of a colt; for she never seemed to know what to do with her long limbs, which were very much in her way. She had a decided mouth, a comical nose, and sharp, grey eyes, which appeared to see everything, and were by turns fierce, funny or thoughtful. Her long, thick hair was her one beauty; but it was usually bundled into a net, to be out of her way. Round shoulders had Jo, big hands and feet, a fly-away look to her clothes, and the uncomfortable appearance of a girl who was rapidly shooting up into a young woman and didn't like it.

Elizabeth . . . or Beth, as everyone called her . . . was a rosy, smooth-haired, bright-eyed girl of 13, with a shy manner, a timid voice, and a peaceful expression, which was seldom disturbed. Her father called her "Little Tranquillity," and the name suited her excellently; for she seemed to live in a happy world of her own, only venturing out to meet the few she trusted and loved.

Amy, though the youngest, was a most important person . . . in her own opinion at least. A regular snow-maiden, with blue eyes, and yellow hair, curling on her shoulders, pale and slender, and always carrying herself like a young lady, unmindful of her manners.*

*Louisa May Alcott, *Little Women*.

Today's Quote: *I don't believe that the accident of birth makes people sisters or brothers. It makes them siblings. Gives them mutuality of parentage. Sisterhood and brotherhood is a condition people have to work at.* — Maya Angelou

Today's Verse: Then Rachel said, "I have had a great struggle with my sister, and I have won" (Gen. 30:8).

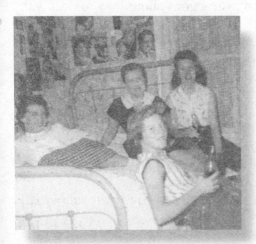

Those who tease you,
love you.
Jewish proverb

Day 11
Real Friends

A lady writes: My sister is a police officer in Los Angeles. Before she was to be commissioned, there were all kinds of training exercises which she had to pass before she became a real policeperson. Further, they were to be trained in how to react and act as an officer. While attending the academy, where they were being trained in all kinds of procedures in every conceivable situation in which they may find themselves confronted while on duty, one procedure surprised her. They were given training and instructions about how to deal with snakebite victims.

Then this training took a more serious twist as the instructor gave them directions about what to do for oneself if bitten by a poisonous snake and unable to get to medical attention quickly. He talked about not running, but resting, about remaining calm, of preparation, and so forth. He went on to explain in great detail that in some extreme circumstances, one would have to cut the skin with a sharp knife and suck the venom out by mouth.

At this point, my sister asked, "What happens if I get bitten on my behind?"

There was a long moment of silence, then the instructor answered, "You find out if you have any friends."

KEEP HER GRIT

Hang on! Cling on! No matter what they say.
Push on! Sing on! Things will come your way.
Sitting down and whining never helps a bit;
Best way to get there is by keeping up your grit.

Don't give up hoping when the ship goes down,
Grab a spar or something . . . just refuse to drown.
Don't think you're dying because you're hit.
Smile in the face of danger and hang on to your grit.

Folks die too easy . . . they sort of fade away,
Make a little error, and give up in dismay.
Kind of woman that's needed is the woman of ready wit,
To laugh at pain and trouble and keep her grit.

(Unknown)

Today's Quote: *Life in common among people who love each other is the ideal of happiness.* — George Sand

Today's Verse: A cheerful heart is good medicine, but a crushed spirit dries up the bones (Prov. 17:22).

Day 12
The Best

When Mary Douglas was a missionary in India she did all within her power to evangelize everyone. But of greatest concern to her were her immediate neighbors, most of whom were Hindus.

One morning she spoke to a woman, a neighbor of hers, walking past her house pulling two of her children in a wagon. One child was clear-eyed, alert, lovely, and the picture of a healthy child. The other was quite seriously deformed and sat in the wagon with a dull stare in his eyes, no change of expression, unresponsive. In their very brief conversation the Hindu woman said, "I'm on my way to the temple by the river to make a sacrifice to the gods 'for my sins.' "

Mrs. Douglas quickly spoke of Jesus Christ and His sacrifice on the cross for all of humanity, even for Hindi women, but she would not listen and hurried on with her two children and the wagon.

Some days later she happened to see the Hindu woman coming again down the street pulling the same wagon. Mary stopped by the road and greeted the woman warmly as she approached. In the wagon on this day there was only one child, the deformed one. In an attempt to make conversation, Mary asked, "Where is your other child?"

"Don't you remember?" answered the woman. "I told you I was going to make a sacrifice. I offered my other child by throwing him into the river."

Mrs. Douglas was horrified, "How could you do that? And if you had to give up one of your sons, why didn't you sacrifice this crippled one and spare the healthy one?"

The Hindu woman squinted in the bright sunshine, then looking Mrs. Douglas in the eye said, "I don't know how it is in your religion, but in our religion, we give our best."

Sobering . . . in fact, even jarring. We don't like to think about such things. Could a person really do that? What really is important to us? What would we be willing to give our very best for? Perhaps this is the moment to stop and think it through. Where are the real priorities of living? Is it in our relationship to God or to self? In every life there has to be a bottom line, someplace. In establishing your priorities, a working thought would be, "With whom or what will I spend the longest time?" It goes without saying that, hopefully, the longest of all relationships will be with God, the Creator. The next longest will be with your own self, followed by family members, and so forth. It's a place to start, to give some serious thought. To what am I willing to give my best?

Today's Quote: *The gauge of what we would do is determined by what we actually do with what we have.*

Today's Verse: From everyone who has been given much, much will be demanded; and from the one who has been entrusted with much, much more will be asked (Luke 12:48).

Day 13
Sisters of Fortune

It is said that tragedy brings siblings together like nothing else ever could. Such was the case with the three Fortune sisters — Ethel, Alice, and Mabel — who survived the sinking of the *Titanic* on the night of April 14–15, 1912. Although the girls were young, the horror of the event remained in their memories.

As ship's officers and crew scrambled frantically to fill lifeboats, Mrs. Mark Fortune stood on the deck with her husband. Their son, Charles, stood nearby. Mark Fortune assured his wife that he and the boy would find passage on another ship or lifeboat. However, the word had passed rather quickly that any rescue would probably come too late. Most of the men knew this and urged their wives to scramble aboard boats. Many women refused.

As the Fortune family huddled on the slanting decks, one of the girls called out to Charles to "take care of Father." Finally, the ladies entered the creaking lifeboat and were dropped into the inky darkness below, settled in for a four-hour journey on the choppy waves of the North Atlantic. Toward dawn, the rescue ship *Carpathia* steamed into view and fired rockets.

Upon stepping onto the deck of *Carpathia*, the girls and their mother discovered that Mark and Charles were not among the survivors. The grief on that chilly morning was horrible to see.

History tells us little of the rest of these girls' lives, but you can count on the fact that arguments were few and far between. Tragedy has a way of drawing close those who love each other. Especially sisters. They are better able than most to convey feelings and fears and joy.

Have you and your sister (or sisters) walked through a valley together? Has the experience strengthened you because you didn't have to walk alone? Perhaps your lives together have been richer than they would have been otherwise . . . because of the healing only a sister can bring.

It might be good to remember that the next time you are mad at your sister — or vice versa — that she once dried your tears over a broken romance, or reassured you after the death of a parent. Remembering the bad makes it all good. Tough times make us grateful for each other.*

*Walter Lord, *A Night to Remember* (New York, NY: Henry Holt and Company).

Today's Quote: *I don't believe that life is supposed to make you feel good, or to make you feel miserable either. Life is supposed to make you feel.* — Gloria Naylor

Today's Verse: Where you go I will go, and where you stay I will stay. Your people will be my people and your God my God. Where you die I will die, there I will be buried (Ruth 1:16–17).

Day 14
Always Old

To all of us, Hannah and Aggie had always been "old." None of us remember a time when they were not "old." In retrospect, it seems that these two sisters have always been somewhere languishing in their senior years. It's now a mystery, but somehow they must have made the leap in time from girlhood to senior citizens without any kind of transition in between. They've always been old to the rest of us and just part of our little town, the Swenson sisters.

Another remarkable thing that comes to mind is that very rarely were they ever seen without the other. It seems to me that there might have been a short break when Hannah first married her husband Gus, and then Aggie married James. That was a short period because Gus died of some mysterious sickness and Hannah moved back to the "home place." Quite shortly after that, they tell us, Aggie and James also moved into the same house. There were some children, it seems to me. I seem to recall that Hannah and Gus parented twin daughters, but that's kind of fuzzy. Then, James also died — cancer, they say. So Hannah and Aggie lived alone together in the same house.

Times did change, however, I'm told. Their house became the place where the quilting circle began to meet.

There was talk of these Swenson sisters being placed in a nursing home in the later years . . . but it never happened. Hannah went first nd the very next day Aggie died, too. The local funeral director and preacher were left to make the decisions as none of their children ared enough to come back home, not even to check the wills. There vas nothing left except that old ramshackle, falling-down mysterious louse. It sold on auction.

To the rest of us, their lives seemed to amount to nothing but peculation. What had they done to make our town a better place? Vhat had they contributed in life? Nothing we could think of. Nothing . . . except having provided company for each other.

Today's Quote: *The choice is quite simple . . . you can either stand up nd be counted or lie down and be counted out.*

Today's Verse: Behold, I am coming soon! My reward is with me, and will to everyone according to what he has done (Rev. 22:12).

Often in old age, they become each other's chosen and most happy companions. In addition to their shared memories of childhood . . . they share memories of the same home, the same homemaking style, and the same small prejudices about housekeeping that carry the echoes of their mother's voice.

Margaret Mead

Day 15
Nothing This Family Can't Do

The day was brilliantly sunny. A snowstorm had passed . . . the phone rang. The news was not good. My father was in the hospital. He'd had a stroke. It was like a replay of that awful day six years earlier when I'd received the news about Mommy.

Daddy slipped into a coma and never regained consciousness. With a little smile on his face as though he were going to meet his dear Tass, Daddy died on February 15, 1983, a month short of his 58th birthday.

This time the undertaker did not suggest that we hire pallbearers but simply assumed that Donald's daughters would carry him to his grave as we had carried our mother.

Could we manage it? We were older. Daddy was heavier. We resolved our doubts the same way we had before, by telling one another, "Women can do anything they put their minds to."

Gathered in the house that Daddy'd built and we'd grown up in, we talked about what we wanted to say at his service. Here we were: Betty, a nurse; Donna, a court reporter; Linda, a dentist; Rita, the head of the science department in a private school; Jeanette and I, both doctors. Independent women, women capable of taking care of themselves.

"How did he do it?" I mused aloud. "How did Daddy turn out six women like us?"

"Daddy was the bow and we were the arrows," someone said. "And he aimed high."

It called to mind the gospel according to Daddy, starting with: "If you're a musician, they can break your fingers. If you're an athlete, they can break your kneecaps. But . . . " Here he always paused dramatically. "*But,* if you are educated, once you've got something in your head, it's yours as long as you live."

And there was: "If the door doesn't open, climb through a window. If the window is closed, try to get in through the cellar. If that's locked, go up on the roof and see if you can get in through the chimney. There is always a way if you keep trying."

We spoke most of all of his single-minded devotion to his family. "If loving my family is wrong," he often said, "then I don't want to be right." He was right, with a wisdom all his own.

At the cemetery we lifted the flag-draped coffin. As determined then as during his life not to let our father down, the ditchdigger's daughters delivered him, without a stumble, to his grave beside Tass, his beloved wife.*

*Yvonne S. Thornton, *The Ditchdigger's Daughters* (New York, NY: Birch Lane Press, Carol Publishing Group, 1995), as it appeared in *Reader's Digest,* September 1995.

Today's Quote: *Women can do anything.* — Five Thornton Sisters

Today's Verse: I can do everything through him who gives me strength (Phil. 4:13).

Day 16
It Is Well . . .

It's 1873 and Horatio Spafford, a Christian attorney from Chicago, had booked passage for his wife and four children, all sisters, on the luxury liner *Ville de Havre* sailing out of New York to France. Spafford himself anticipated joining them on their vacation holiday in about three or four weeks, after finishing some business. Except for his wife, he never saw them again.

The trip had a wonderful start . . . but on the evening of November 21, in mid-Atlantic, the luxury liner was struck by another ship, the *Lochearn*, and sank in less than 30 minutes, taking most of the passengers to their death.

On being warned that the ship was sinking, Mrs. Spafford knelt with her children and prayed that they might be saved or be made willing to die, if such would be God's will. In the confusion, three of the children were swept away by the waves while she stood clutching the youngest. Then she, too, was swept from her arms. Mrs. Spafford was struck by some of the debris and knocked unconscious. She awoke later to find that she had been rescued by some sailors from the *Lochearn*. But the four sisters were gone.

Back in the United States, Horatio Spafford was waiting for news of his family. It was 10 days later, after the rescue ship had sailed to Cardiff, Wales, that the message came. "Saved alone" was his wife's message. That night Spafford walked the floor of his home in anguish. His only recourse was to pray as he shared his loss with His Lord. Later he told his friend, Major Whittle, "I am glad to be able to trust my Lord when it costs me something." Sometime later, as he reflected back on the personal disaster at sea, he wrote this hymn.

> *When peace, like a river, attendeth my way,*
> *When sorrows like sea-billows roll;*
> *Whatever my lot, Thou hast taught me to say,*
> *It is well, it is well with my soul.*
>
> *Though Satan should buffet, though trials should come,*
> *Let this blest assurance control,*
> *That Christ has regarded my helpless estate,*
> *And hath shed His own blood for my soul. . . .*
>
> *And, Lord, haste the day when the faith shall be sight,*
> *The clouds be rolled back as a scroll,*
> *The trump shall resound and the Lord shall descend,*
> *"Even so" . . . it is well with my soul.*

Today's Quote: *Do not follow where the path may lead. Follow God, instead, where there is no path and leave a trail.*

Today's Verse: For God did not appoint us to suffer wrath but to receive salvation through our Lord Jesus Christ (1 Thess. 5:9).

Day 17
Sharing the Bad News . . . Gently

A woman was called out of town on a business trip and she asked her sister to take care of her cat for her while she was away. The cat happened to be one of those beautiful, registered, show quality Siamese cats. This cat meant everything to the woman. She made sure the cat had the very best of everything which included food, care, and exercise. The cat was a show-stopper — gorgeous and very pampered.

The problem was that the sister didn't really like cats at all.

The first thing the woman did upon completing her business trip was to call her sister's house and inquire about her cat. The sister was curt, blunt, and to the point when she replied, "Your cat died." And then she hung up on her sister.

For the next few hours and on into the next day, the woman was inconsolable in her grief. She called her sister back and said, "We have to talk, I'm coming right over."

When she arrived at her sister's home, obviously hurt, she pointed out, "It was needlessly cruel and sadistic of you to tell me so bluntly that my poor prize-winning cat had passed away. It was almost more of a shock than I could stand."

The sister then demanded, "Well, what did you expect me to do?"

She replied, "Well . . . you at least could have broken the bad news to me gradually. First, you could have said my cat was playing on the roof. Later you could have called to say that she had fallen off. Then the next morning you could have called and said something about the fact that one of her legs was broken. Then, when I came to get her, you could have told me how she had passed away in the middle of the night."

Her sister, nodded, understandingly, and said, "Okay, I'm getting the drift."

She went on, then, "But, it's too bad that you didn't have enough civility to treat me like your grown-up adult sister. I will, however, forgive you this time, though I don't know how I'll get along without my wonderful cat."

The sister, then, out of concern, responded, "I'm so sorry. In the future I will keep your suggestions in mind. Please forgive me."

"You're forgiven. Oh, by the way, how is Mama doing?"

Her sister pondered, thoughtfully, momentarily, then announced, "Mama is playing on the roof."

Today's Quote: *Taken from a sign on a convent in Southern California: "Absolutely No Trespassing. Violators Will Be Prosecuted to the Full Extent of the Law. Signed, 'The Sisters of Mercy.' "*

Today's Verse: Now Sarah was listening at the entrance to the tent, which was behind him. Abraham and Sarah were already old and well advanced in years, and Sarah was past the age of child-bearing. So Sarah laughed to herself as she thought . . .
(Gen. 18:10–12).

Day 18
A Potpourri on Sisterhood

I can't think I had much of a sense of humor as long as I remained the only child. When my brother Edward came along after I was three, we both became comics, making each other laugh. We set each other off, as we did for life, from the minute he learned to talk. A sense of the absurd was communicated between us probably before that. — Eudora Welty

All older children feel that they are "not good enough" when a younger sibling is born. Not, somehow, "up to snuff." They come to feel that somehow they were born a "Ford Pinto," and are in effect being "recalled by the manufacturer." Maybe you tried to look closely at the face of your sister at birth, and it looked like a stewed grape, and you thought, *This is an improvement?* — Stephanie Brush

Not being kissed at 16 was harder for me to endure than it otherwise would have been because Ramona, my 12-year-old sister, had been. She had had boy friends since she was 10. She had big boys of 15 hanging around her from whom I would have been proud to have a glance. They treated me like Ramona's old-maid aunt. My brother Neddie was only 16 months younger than I. When we were together where people didn't know us, I sidled up to him in a way I hoped onlookers would think romantic. To this day, Neddie still sits across the room from me when we visit. That year of sidling has made him permanently wary. — Jessamyn West

But however you might rebel, there was no shedding them. They were your responsibility and there was no one to relieve you of them. They called you "Sis." All your life people called you Sis, because that was what you were, or what you became — big sister, helpful sister, the one upon whom everyone depended, the one they all came to for everything from help with homework to a sliver under the fingernail. — Wallace Stegner

Celestine and Hortense had been drawn closely together in affection since they had come to live under the same roof, and they formed virtually one household. The two sisters-in-law stayed at home and looked after their children together, and this had created a bond between them. They had come to be so close to each other that they spoke their thoughts aloud. They presented a touching picture of two sisters in harmony — one happy, the other sad. Perhaps the contrast between them contributed to their warm friendship: each found in the other what she lacked in herself. — Honor'e de Balzac

Today's Quote: *Sisterhood is powerful.* — Robin Morgan

Today's Verse: Naomi said to Ruth her daughter-in-law, "It will be good for you, my daughter, to go with his girls, because in someone else's field you might be harmed" (Ruth 2:22).

Day 19
Little Sisters

"Wanna play dress up, Cheriee? I'm gonna be the mommy and the television model and be real rich and famous."

"Then I wanna be a doctor, a baby doctor, and have a hospital and lots of nurses and have lots of babies."

"Okay. You get to wear the all-white dress 'cause I wore it last time. Those shoes aren't doctor shoes, those are too high. You'll only fall down. Try these. These are much gooder, these are white."

"Then, Susan, you live in a mansion with a pool. I live in a brick house. I'm gonna get in my convertible and drive over to visit you."

"You should fly 'cause you got lots of money. You're flying to visit me 'cause we're sisters and we need to visit and we haven't done it in a long time and we're unhappy 'cause we miss each other 'cause sisters get together and talk real often."

"I'll fly in a big jet and we'll meet at the airport and we'll give each other big hugs, because sisters always hug, 'specially at airports and things. It makes me feel good when I hug you and you hug me."

"But, Mommy hugs are better. Sister hugs are next."

"Susan, that's not fair. We're kids and sisters and we're playing grown-up. No fair. We will be mommies some time, but not now."

"But Mommy is a grown-up, you're a kid, and I'm a kid. That doesn't mean I don't like your hugs, either."

"Then I don't like your hugs, either, silly."

"Oh, silly. I like and really looove your hugs. See, now, I'm hugging you real tight."

" I'm tired of playing models and doctors and dress up."

"Now I get to choose. Let's play house."

"No. You always get to be the mommie."

"Then, let's play shopping."

"No, 'cause you always make me push the cart and carry the groceries and things. You always get to pay the money."

"Okay, then, now, let's have a tea party."

Today's Quote: *"Girls" is what women over 45 call each other.*

Today's Verse: Treat younger men as brothers, older women as mothers, and younger women as sisters, with absolute purity (1 Tim. 5:1–2).

*Freedom is the positive possession
of only those sisters who have the
courage to defend it.*

Anonymous

Day 20
Bigger Than Winning

They are remembered simply, sadly, as "The Falls." They are among the most poignant moments of Olympic history.

During the 1988 Winter Games in Calgary, Dan Jansen, a gold medal favorite, came out on the ice to skate the 500 meters only hours after learning that his sister had died of leukemia. As he rounded the first turn, the weight of the agonizing news seemed to crush him to the ice. Four days later Jansen tried again in the 1,000 . . . and again he fell, this time on a straightaway.

"It was very hard realizing that all my accomplishments didn't seem to matter, that all I would be known for was falling in the Olympics," he says. He needed time just to believe "that it wasn't going to happen again."

Since then Jansen has matured and married . . . and emerged, ready for another run for the gold.

Since winning the 1988 World Sprint Championships on his home turf (ice) in West Allis, Wisconsin, he's been America's most consistent male speed skater. In 1991–92 Jansen skated stride for stride in the 500 with defending Olympic gold-medalist Uwe-Jens Mey and broke the German's world record.

Yet Calgary forever altered his life perspective. Jansen soberly said, "Losing a sister was a lot bigger deal than winning a medal could ever be. Winning the gold can never again be the most important thing in my life."*

The 1994 Olympics from Norway are now history, and it appeared to be deja vu over again as Dan Jansen fell in the 500 meter event, then it happened again in the 1,000 meters sprint. There was only one event left for Dan to skate in . . . 1,500 meters. This was not his best sprint distance. Remember, he was the world record holder in the 500. It was to be his last race in his last Olympic competition! We were riveted to our TV sets as the drama unfolded for us. The gun sounded. Dan, as he had promised, gave his very best . . . setting a time which held up to win his last race! It was one of those special times!

On the awards stand, as the gold medal was placed around his neck, we watched the emotion. As our national anthem was played there were tears . . . then a salute given heavenward. This race was in honor of his sister . . . and we recalled his life-priority, "Winning the gold can never again be the most important thing in my life."

*Newsweek, 2/10/92.

Today's Quote: *The only time you can't afford to fail is the last time you try.* — Charles Kettering.

Today's Verse: Do you not know that in a race all the runners run, but only one gets the prize? Run in such a way as to get the prize (1 Cor. 9:24).

Day 21
Sister as a Confidante

Consider the relationship between Terri, 34, and her sister Catherine, 37, who recently spent a quiet weekend together after Catherine's second miscarriage. During the weekend, Catherine talked about her immediate concerns, including her difficulty in getting pregnant and keeping the pregnancy, and her worry about her "biological clock" and her desire for a child. She needed the calming reassurance of a friend, and Terri had seemed like an obvious choice because she, too, had lost her own first baby when she was five months pregnant.

Initially, Terri had not been supportive of Catherine's efforts to become pregnant, because she had thought that Catherine was taking too much of a physical risk. Years earlier, she had tried to influence Catherine to have children when she was younger, before she had established her professional life. But Catherine had decided to wait, and now, although she did not regret her decision, she needed to discuss its ramifications with someone she trusted, someone other than her husband.

Fortunately, Terri proved to be the perfect choice. She listened actively and empathetically. She became a sounding board for Catherine's questions, tears, and convictions. By the end of the weekend, Catherine was sure she had found a friend in her sister . . . a non-judgmental, reassuring listener who would ease the decision-making process for her.*

Communication is the life-blood of sisterhood. This has been defined in terms of the messages we send within the context of who and what we are. When sisters send messages, often it is filtered through the remembered events of childhood, so the response may be garbled by an event of the past. In communicating with an adult sister, it's most helpful to remember that she is no longer a little girl. She, too, is grown up with a life of her own. Look behind the message to discover the motivation which may have prompted the current exchange. To solve communication differences may take a greater effort to learn how to reflect, how to discover the very essence of a problem, to become an active listener, and to be non-judgmental.

Maybe your sister has leveled the accusation: "You just don't hear what I have to say!" which is a signal that all is not as it should be in this area. Make the conscious decision to commit to the effort to improve, not simply to "fake" it. Perhaps it's time for sisters to clear away some of the rubble of the past and move on to develop realistic, positive expectations from this communication interaction. Commit to better communications to improve your sister relationship.

*Dale V. Atkins, *Sisters* (New York, NY: Arbor House Pub. Co., 1984), p. 67.

Today's Quote: *A true sister is a friend who listens with her heart.*
— Unknown

Today's Verse: Apply your heart to instruction and your ears to words of knowledge (Prov. 23:12).

Day 22
Why Are We Here?

Corrie Ten Boom writes: One day in the concentration camp, I was very encouraged because I was told I was free to go. I stood before the gate and I knew: as soon as this gate opens, I am free. In this concentration camp I had been able to bring the gospel to many women. A great number died with the name of Jesus on their lips. The Lord had used my sister Betsie and me to show them the way.

Here I was, standing before the gate. My sister had died about two weeks earlier. While I stood there waiting, somebody came to me and said, "Corrie, I must tell you something. Today Mrs. de Boer and Mrs. de Goede both died."

I looked at this cruel camp for the last time, and I said, "Thank You, Lord, that You brought me here, even if only for these two women who were saved for eternity. You used Betsie and me to that end. Lord, if it were only for these two women, it was worth all our suffering, even Betsie's death." It is worth living and dying if we are being used to save others for eternity. You and I can be used, whoever we are.*

Once again, we are faced with the question: Why are we here? If you are a Christian, the plan for your life is quite simple and clear. We have been commissioned to share — the challenge reads like this: "You are the salt of the earth. . . . You are the light of the world. . . . Go and make disciples" (Matt. 5:13–14, 28:19).

If you are not a Christian, the plan is forthright: To become a Christian. How? The Bible challenges you to believe in your heart and confess with your mouth. The promise was expressed by Jesus Christ in John 3:16 when He said that God so loved this world that He sent His only Son as a sacrifice to take away the sins of the world, including yours.

God has planned that this world would have an ongoing witness. People who, like a mirror, reflect the person and presence of the Lord Jesus Christ to others around us. He wants to live through each of us in such a way that others are also challenged to live for Him and change the world around us. Perhaps your commission will be to take this message of the gospel to your sister if she is not a believer, to live it for your sister, to pray for your sister, to sacrifice for your sister, to love your sister into the kingdom of heaven.

Why are we here? To become part of the family of God and to share the good news that it is possible for others to also become part of God's family. This is the family relationship that lasts for eternity!

*Corrie ten Boom, *Not I, But Christ* (Nashville, TN: Thomas Nelson Publishers, 1983), p. 61.

Today's Quote: *Lord, I thank You . . . we all thank You . . . that You want to use us for this great work. Light must be spread, and You want to use us.* — Corrie ten Boom

Today's Verse: Again Jesus said, "Peace be with you! As the Father has sent me, I am sending you" (John 20:21).

Day 23
Mary and Salome

Mary, the mother of Jesus, was referred to by the Jews as the daughter of Eli; but early Christian writers called her the daughter of Joakim and Anna. She was related by marriage to Elizabeth, the wife of Zacharias, the priest.

Salome, most biblical scholars agree, was the name of the beloved disciple's (John) mother . . . but further conjecture, on quite reliable grounds, states that she was the sister of Mary. Very little is written about her in the Gospel narratives. What is evident is that she, like her two sons John and James, was a very devoted follower of Jesus and was present at the Crucifixion and assisted at His entombment.

We can only speculate about the sister relationship between Mary and Salome. What did this sister do when Mary announced that she was pregnant by the Holy Spirit?

Perhaps no other mother in history has suffered so long or so intensely in long travail for her son as Mary did in deep concern for Jesus from His conception, His birth in Bethlehem, to the final tragic night on Golgotha. Mary, we can also assume, was marked by profound thoughtfulness and a maternal kind of love. This is indicated in the biblical passage which says that, "His mother kept all these things in her heart." I tend to picture Salome as being the more happy, the more out-going, the bubbly one of these two sisters. Do you think they laughed together? Can you imagine what some of their sister-to-sister talks would have covered? It's so hard for us to see the human side of such awesome biblical people, especially Mary. Have you wondered who would have been her support system? My premise is that her own sister, her own flesh and blood, Salome, was there to listen, to comfort, to pray with, and encourage. Even at the foot of the Cross when Jesus committed his mother to the care of John, His beloved disciple, by saying, "Mary, behold your son," and to John, "Behold your mother." The Bible indicates that Salome would have been there, too!

Today's Quote: *Family faces are magic mirrors. Looking at people who belong to us, we see the past, present and future.* — Gail Lumet Buckley

Today's Verse: In the sixth month, God sent the angel Gabriel to Nazareth . . . to a virgin pledged to be married to a man named Joseph, a descendant of David. The virgin's name was Mary (Luke 1:26–27). Many women were there, watching from a distance. They had followed Jesus from Galilee to care for his needs. Among them were Mary Magdalene, Mary the mother of James and Joses, and the mother of Zebedee's sons (Matt. 27:55–56).

Day 24
Inseparable

Grace looked forward to the birth of the baby. Although her mother and father cautioned her against hoping too hard, Grace just knew she would have a sister. They would have teas together, read books about faraway princes and princesses, and do a thousand other things in the years ahead. They would be inseparable.

The months disappeared slowly for Grace. Finally, weeks from Christmas, the day came. But as her father hurried past her one morning, Grace became aware that several people were in the house, and none of them looked happy. Didn't they realize her mother needed absolute quiet?

Hours later, the sad-faced doctor emerged from Mother's bedroom. He spoke in a low voice to Father, then left the room. Dread came upon Grace, and she no longer thought about teas and fairy tales.

At the cemetery, Grace was aware of only a few things: steam from the horse's nostrils as the animals waited impatiently in the cold December air; and Mother's forlorn expression as she sat stiffly in the carriage. Many people spoke to the family, but Grace wasn't listening.

Years later, when Grace was having her own baby, she was naturally anxious. After the birth, she asked for the nurse who had held her hand and reassured her in the early morning hours when labor had started. *"We have no such woman here,"* said the director of nursing.

When Grace was 50, she received alarming news that her son was missing in action during the Allied invasion of Europe. Two agonizing months went by before word came — he was safe! Grace's son would have been added to the casualty list were it not for a courageous local who hid him in a cellar while enemy troops ransacked her farm. Later, Red Cross attempts to contact her turned up nothing.

Twenty years later, on the night of her husband's death, Grace held his hand in those last hours. Feeling so alone in the empty house, she finally drifted off to sleep. Oddly refreshed, she awoke to the sweet fragrance of her favorite tea, steaming in a cup by the bedside.

And two weeks past her 85th birthday, Grace felt her time drawing near. As she lay upstairs, a spring breeze fluttered the curtains. Grace closed her eyes, and an oddly-familiar hand grasped hers. Those who attended the funeral commented on her sweet smile.

Do you believe loved ones we've never known have no place in our hearts? Or do you believe that when the veil is finally lifted, we will enjoy reunions that only an omniscient Creator could provide? Make up your own mind, but I know what I believe!

Today's Quote: *Faith has to do with things that are not seen, and hope with things that are not in hand.* — Saint Thomas Aquinas

Today's Verse: See that you do not look down on one of these little ones. For I tell you that their angels in heaven always see the face of my Father in heaven (Matt. 18:10).

Day 25
A Letter to a Sister

Salem, Jan 15, 1767

Dear Sister,
Your kind letter I receiv'd today
and am greatly rejoiced to (hear) you are all so well.
I was very uneasy at not hearing from you,
indeed my dear Sister the Winter never seem'd
so tedious to me in the World.
I daily count the days between this and the time
I may probably see you.
I could never feel so comfortable as I at present do,
if I thought I should spend another Winter here.
Indeed my Sister I cannot bear the thought
of staying here so far from all my Friends if
Mr. Cranch can do as well nigher.
I would give a great deal only to know I was
within Ten Miles of you if I could not see you.
Our children will never seem so natural to each other
as if they liv'd where they could see one another oftener. . . .

(This letter was written from Mary Smith Cranch to her sister,
Abigail Adams.)

Today's Quote: *Men live by forgetting . . . women live on memories.* — T. S. Eliot

Today's Verse: Everyone who quotes proverbs will quote this proverb about you: "Like mother, like daughter." You are a true daughter of your mother . . . and you are a true sister of your sisters (Ezek. 16:44–45).

A woman should always stand by a woman.

Euripides

Day 26
Sister Wishes

Carol and Helen didn't like the same foods, clothes, boys, books... well, you get the idea. But these sisters loved each other with a heavenly love. Throughout childhood, they played a silly game called "I wish for you." More often than not, good things did come their way.

Carol and Helen stayed close when graduation sent one of them away from home. Carol married and had children. Helen remained single and found fulfillment in the advertising world of Madison Avenue.

Years passed. One day, the day Carol found the lump, she instinctively ran to call "Sis." Through a long distance line and many tears, the sisters comforted one another.

The doctor was very up front: Cancer. Carol was stoic, even upbeat. In the still of the night, Carol curled up on the couch and called Helen. By the next afternoon, they were meeting at the airport.

Helen's visit became indefinite. As the weeks slipped by, so did Carol's hope. Oh, she tried to be her old funny self. "Cancer Carol and Healthy Helen," she'd say. But the prognosis wasn't good. When the tears came, Helen learned that Carol was fearful only for her family.

On a crisp December morning Helen returned from a pre-dawn walk. Carol grabbed her arm. "I'm scared," she admitted. Helen was very positive, strangely reassuring. She didn't even cry.

That evening, Helen suddenly announced she was going home. Carol blinked. How could she leave *now*? Carol assumed Helen had reached a point where she could no longer deal with a terminal sister.

At the airport, Helen embraced her sister and put a hand to her cheek. They said very little, just the usual goodbyes.

Waiting for her doctor one day, Carol gazed at one of the office paintings. Two little girls walking hand-in-hand through a meadow. Carol closed her eyes and could almost smell the wildflowers.

"Carol," the doctor said as he eased into the room. "I'll just tell you right now that we can't find any cancer from these tests. It's gone, and I have no explanation. You're cancer-free."

Jumping up the front steps in one leap, Carol burst through the door. She had good news, she told her grim-faced husband. "But I have bad news, honey. It's Helen. She was in a car accident today, and I'm afraid. . . . " His voice trailed off but Carol knew. And the rest of the evening, indeed, the rest of their lives, was bittersweet.

So, what is your speculation on this story? What do you think Helen did on her morning walk? I like to think she did a little bargaining with someone. Someone who had the power to grant wishes. Fervent wishes. Sister wishes.

Today's Quote: *Self-sacrifice is never entirely unselfish, for the giver never fails to receive.* — Dolores E. McGuire

Today's Verse: Greater love has no one than this, that he lay down his life for his friends (John 15:13).

Day 27
To My Sister

To My Sister

My sister! ('tis a wish of mine)
Now that our morning meal is done,
Make haste, your morning task resign;
Come forth and feel the sun.

One moment now may give us more
Than years of toiling reason;
Our minds shall drink at every pore
The spirit of the season.

Then come, my Sister! Come I pray,
With speed put on your woodland dress;
And bring no book: for this one day
We'll give to idleness.
— William Wordsworth

There is a very special kind of freedom that sisters enjoy. In fact, this sister-to-sister relationship may be the envy of all other kinds of human relationships. Sisters seem to have discovered the freedom to share their innermost thoughts without fear. There is a freedom to ask personal favors, favors which may greatly inconvenience the other sister, but nevertheless, it's this freedom which allows the question to be asked, the favor to be expected. Sisters have no problems in sharing their true feelings, feelings which are intimate and personal, revealing hidden inner thoughts which could be revealed to no one else, but it seems right and true that they should be shared with a sister who in turn will guard those feelings as Fort Knox guards our gold.

Perhaps most special about the sister relationship is the freedom to totally and completely be themselves — no put on, no pretense, no cover-up, no fear of being put down. This luxury of being able to simply be yourself is a fantastic benefit.

Sisterhood is more than just being a sister. It's wonderful to have each other as sisters, but the joy goes beyond to becoming and continuing to be the very best of friends. Many sisters will freely confess the blessings of being and having a sister but the real celebration is that here, too, is the very best of all best friends.

Today's Quote: *It is only the women whose eyes have been washed clear with tears who get the broad vision that makes them little sisters to all the world.* — Dorothy Dix

Today's Verse: Pointing to his disciples, he said, "Here are my mother and my brothers. For whoever does the will of my Father in heaven is my brother and sister and mother" (Matt. 12:49–50).

Day 28
To Be a Sister

Elizabeth Fishel expresses it like this: "The desire to be and have a sister is a primitive and profound one that may have everything or nothing to do with the family a woman is born to. It is a desire to know and be known by someone who shares blood and body, history and dreams, common ground and the unknown adventures of the future, darkest secrets and the glassiest beads of truth."

Well what do you do if you weren't born a sister and still have this "desire" to be a sister? You simply go in search of that sister who can become blood and body, history and dreams. Merlene and Donna fit this scenario, each being born last into a family composed of only brothers — Merlene has two, Donna has three. As time and fate would have it, Merlene and her family moved next door to Donna and her family. Soon it was coffee over the back fence. This soon moved on to longer heart-to-heart chats. Before long a bond began to form which was more than two women sharing friendship.

This relationship was cultivated with morning constitutional walks, lots of coffee times, some cries together, to move into a relationship that was more sister-like than being good neighbors. Soon it was nicknames — "B.B." for Merlene and "Donn" for Donna. Then separation came with Merlene off to California. It was then that the realization struck . . . life would never quite be the same without each other. The long distance phone bills were something else. Distance deepened this sister type of relationship. Soon it was not only phone bills . . . it was airfares between California and the midwest . . . the midwest and California.

Time continued to season this sisterhood. Soon came the realization that if it were to last, effort must be invested. Then there were vacations together . . . couples with spouses, to the Caribbean, and an auto trip up the West Coast to Vancouver and more. Then job opportunities changed . . . circumstances allowed Merlene to move from California to Missouri. Soon these two were working at the same place for the same ministry. While a home was being hunted, the two families lived together.

This relationship . . . Merlene and Donna, salt and pepper, night and day differences, has endured family tragedies, distance, spouses, crisis with kids and grandkids, until the decision has been made to make every effort to grow old together . . . sisters who may not share the same blood and body or history, but who now share the unknown adventures of the future, secrets which are held behind the glassy beads of the future . . . best friends, sisters who have found a relationship of true sisterhood. And life is good when you have a sister!

Today's Quote: *There is no folly equal to that of throwing away friendship, in a world where friendship is so rare.* — Bulwer-Lyton

Today's Verse: When Naomi realized that Ruth was determined to go with her, she stopped urging her (Ruth 1:18).

Day 29
My Older Sister

During my childhood, my older sister Daryl and I shared the back seat of our parents' white Chevrolet on weekend family outings . . . but an imaginary line divided the seat into separate, hostile camps. If Daryl's arm or leg strayed onto my turf, or vice versa, the car was immediately transformed into a battle zone, with bickering and shouting that even a game of States or Capitals couldn't silence.

But as clearly as I can recall these skirmishes, I can also remember quite different experiences with Daryl during these outings. Late at night, coming home from holiday dinners at our aunt's home just hours after one of our quarrels, my eyelids would become heavy and I'd snuggle next to Daryl and rest my head on her lap. The imaginary dividing line forgotten, she would gently stroke my hair and twirl my pony tail, and often I would feel so close to her that I'd try to fight off sleep to savor the moment. My big sister was taking care of me. These are among my warmest memories of childhood.

Today, three decades later, many of these elements endure in my relationship with Daryl. She is my dear friend, my ally, and although we now live a continent apart, I still look to her for support. Our personal life choices have led us down significantly different paths, but I know that Daryl will always be there when I need her, and I trust that she feels the same about me. Of course, all is not perfect . . . even though the back-seat battles are in the past, our relationship is still tested occasionally by a disagreement or crisis. But we have been strengthened . . . as individuals and as sisters . . . by what we have learned from our childhood experiences.*

Listen to women . . . if they have a sister, good or bad, they all want to talk about this relationship with a sister. Some will reaffirm the positive and the good while others are searching for ways to make it good while looking for answers as to why it's in such disarray.

Sisters can teach more about life than other persons. Sisters can be role models, problem solvers, challengers, socializers, protectors, and caregivers. There is one thing to note about this emotional attachment . . . you meet your sister/sisters in early childhood and given good health, this relationship will outlast your spousal or parental time together. What with 80 or 90 or even more years, this relationship can be the longest lasting of any earthly relationship, other than with yourself. Therefore there is the compelling desire to be unconditionally accepted by one's sister.

*Dale V. Atkins, *Sisters* (New York, NY: Arbor House Pub. Co., 1984), p. 13–14.

Today's Quote: *I wish my daughters the same kind of feelings that their aunts and I have for one another. We are as different as we are close!* — Unknown

Today's Verse: Therefore, as we have opportunity, let us do good to all people, especially to those who belong to the family of believers (Gal. 6:10).

Day 30
Friends, Brothers, and Sisters

The Bible talks about friends, and that friends are to love at all times. It also states that a brother might be/is born for adversity. And most sisters who have brothers might say that those brothers certainly have dished out lots of adversity. But have you ever thought that might not be what the Bible meant with such verses?

But what about a sister? The Bible doesn't talk very much about sisters. What are sisters born for? Why are sisters born? Caroline Burns says, "My sister was born to be the rock of our family. Even before Mother died and Daddy got old, she was the one we depended on."

Sisters are the ones who always remember to send special notes and cards on everybody's birthdays, wedding anniversaries, and all other kinds of occasions to celebrate.

Sisters are the people who love cards, intimate notes, long phone calls, holiday family gatherings, and making sure that nobody is left out.

Sisters are the people who tend to be the glue that holds families together . . . they insist on get-togethers, family reunions, and family gatherings.

Sisters make sure that little sisters and little brothers are always included, whether it is play time when little or going as a family on a special vacation. Sisters are the ones who show to the rest of the siblings what a lady of faith will look like and act like and be like.

Sisters put real life into those old stories we read about the women of the Bible . . . Rachel, Leah, Ruth, Mary, Salome, Deborah, Sarah, and Eve, to name just a few.

Sisters put skin and warmth into those ancient women . . . sisters give us insight into how other families and other women may have been.

Sisters are the natural leader/teachers for younger sisters about how to live life out, simply how to make life work.

Sisters make all of us proud to be family members because sisters remind us of so many things, teach us how to be human, caring, loving, compassionate, and practical.

Shirley Abbott reminds us about all these things as she writes: "Within our family there was no such thing as a person who did not matter. Second cousins thrice removed mattered. We knew . . . and thriftily made use of . . . everybody's middle name. We knew who was buried where. We all mattered, and the dead most of all."*

*Shirley Abbott.

Today's Quote: *A ministering angel shall my sister be.* — Shakespeare

Today's Verse: Likewise, teach the older women to be reverent in the way they live, not to be slanderers or addicted to much wine, but to teach what is good. Then they can train the younger women to love (Titus 2:3–4).